Focus for Success

Strategies for Developing Student Focus in the Classroom and Beyond

Author: Linda Armstrong
Contributor: Amy Armstrong, MS, LPC, NCC
Consultant: Diane Kress Hower, MA, NBCC
Editor: Mary Dieterich
Proofreaders: Alexis Fey and Margaret Brown

COPYRIGHT © 2024 Mark Twain Media, Inc.

ISBN 978-1-62223-895-8

Printing No. CD-405088

Mark Twain Media, Inc., Publishers
Distributed by Carson Dellosa Education

Visit us at www.marktwainpublishing.com

Table of Contents

Table of Contents (cont.)

Introduction: Using This book

Focus is crucial for success. It helps students learn and socialize effectively. It includes thinking skills like:
- goal setting
- planning
- organizing
- attention

It also involves such emotional skills as empathy and impulse control.

Focus for Success offers a variety of practical ways to improve focus. It includes brainstorming pages, graphic organizers, puzzles, mindfulness tools, and journal prompts. It is divided into three parts:

- Part I helps parents deal with focus-related health and environmental concerns.
- Part II addresses such classroom issues as scheduling and note-taking.
- Part III is an interactive workbook for students with puzzles, journal prompts, and practice pages.

The book emphasizes seven ideas:
- patience
- individual differences
- physical activity
- breaks
- pacing
- mindfulness
- communication

Note: *Focus for Success* includes strategies that may help some students with ADD or ADHD. However, these teens, their parents, and teachers need a level of support that falls outside the scope of this work. (Part I does include a page with additional resources.)

Part I: Focus Basics for Parents

Parenting has always been a tough job. Recent events have made raising teens even harder. While this book doesn't have all the answers, it can be a helpful starting point.

Here are some key areas to concentrate on when helping middle schoolers improve their ability to focus:

- **Communication:** Teens rely on friends but still need their parents.

  o This section includes a tool called the Wheel of Emotions to help students discuss their feelings.
  o It also offers suggestions for scheduling family activities. Dinners, movie nights, and shared adventures improve interaction and deepen relationships.

- **Physical Environment:** Middle schoolers need a relaxing, distraction-free study space at home. This part of the book provides tips on setting up a functional work area.

- **Health:** A healthy mind depends on a healthy body. This section includes checklists and charts to address:

  o Vision
  o Hearing
  o Allergies
  o Dental issues

- **Structure:** Daily routines may seem boring but can reduce anxiety. Knowing what to expect can improve a middle schooler's performance, sense of security, and happiness. Part I includes:

  o A sample daily schedule
  o An electronic device usage contract

> Don't forget to check the resources at the end of this section. Most of the books and articles are available through local public libraries.

Growing Pains

Middle school presents special challenges for both students and their parents. Here's a brief overview:

- **Puberty:** Both boys and girls experience powerful changes during adolescence. Hormones affect their bodies and emotions.

  Communication is crucial. Online videos can help parents with "the talk." Check out this option: <https://kidshealth.org/CHOC/en/kids/puberty-normal-video.html>

- **Anxiety and Depression:** Hormonal changes and social challenges make emotional problems more likely. Use the Wheel of Emotions to make it easier to talk about feelings.

  Watch for signs of depression and don't hesitate to get help if needed. <https://www.helpguide.org/articles/depression/parents-guide-to-teen-depression.htm>

- **Neuroplasticity:** Important physical changes occur in teen brains. The frontal lobe and hippocampus grow. Unused neural pathways are pruned away. New ones develop. Communication within the brain improves.

  Learn more about these changes here: <https://www.livescience.com/3435-teen-brains-clear-childhood-thoughts.html>

- **Hormones** during puberty impact mood, behavior, and motivation. These changes make teens vulnerable to high-risk behavior.

  For more information check online resources such as: <https://www.cdc.gov/parents/teens/risk_behaviors.html>

- **Development of Identity:** Adolescence is a time of self-discovery. Middle schoolers begin to define themselves, prioritize their interests, and uncover their unique gifts.

  Check out this interesting article for more: <https://www.edutopia.org/article/encouraging-middle-school-students-embrace-differences/>

The Procrustean Bed: We're All Different

In Greek myth, a thief named Procrustes had a shelter by a road. He invited tired travelers to rest. If someone was too short for his bed, he stretched them to fit. Unfortunately, that treatment was always fatal. If the traveler was too tall, he cut off their legs. That too resulted in death.

A young hero named Theseus killed Procrustes, ending the legendary cruelty. But similar situations exist today. Society often forces people to conform, suppressing their true selves.

Middle school is a time for self-exploration. Tweens develop their own perspectives. They discover interests that differ from those of their families.

As a parent, try to support your child's exploration with extracurricular activities. Make sure middle schoolers are interested before signing them up for lessons. If they want to quit, let them. Quitting is not a loss of focus. It is a healthy part of your teen's process of elimination.

Middle school music, skating, dance, drama, and art lessons are usually not about building a career. They are about enjoying an adventure, making new friends, and gaining experience.

Write down what you want for your child. It can include skills you admire or activities your teen seems talented at, such as music, sports, writing, or art.

____

____

____

____

____

____

____

____

Super Focus: *After the student completes the "What Do I Love?" workbook page on page 30, share this list. Take time to discuss how the two lists are the same and how they differ. Use this discussion to help plan lessons and support. In the end, kids will focus best on what they enjoy.*

Annual Health Checklist

(Keep a hard copy of this form, or something similar, handy.)

Student's Name: ___________________________   Age ______ Grade ______ Year ______

General Practitioner or Pediatrician (Annual Physical)

Doctor: _____________________ Phone: ___________ Address: _______________________

Appt. Date: _______________________   Recommendations: _______________________

Referrals: ____

Follow-up: ____

Insurance Info.: ____

Optical

Doctor: _____________________ Phone: ___________ Address: _______________________

Appt. Date: _______________________   Recommendations: _______________________

Follow-up: ____

Insurance Info.: ____

Dental

Doctor: _____________________ Phone: ___________ Address: _______________________

Appt. Date: _______________________   Recommendations: _______________________

Follow-up: ____

Insurance Info.: ____

Specialist:

Doctor: _____________________ Phone: ___________ Address: _______________________

Appt. Date: _______________________   Recommendations: _______________________

Follow-up: ____

Insurance Info.: ____

Super Focus: *Give tweens time alone with doctors so they can ask personal questions.*

Name:							Date:

The Wheel of Emotions

Help your tween color this diagram with colored pencils. It's a professional tool for discussing feelings. The names of the emotions should still be visible after the wheel is colored.

Directions: Make the sections in the middle of the wheel the brightest. Moving outward, each part should be paler. Each petal point should be a light pastel version of the central color.

The original wheel used the following colors (but you can use others): **Yellow:** serenity, joy, ecstasy; **Yellow-Green:** acceptance, trust, admiration; **Green:** apprehension, fear, terror; **Blue-Green:** distraction, surprise, amazement; **Blue:** pensiveness, sadness, grief; **Purple:** boredom, disgust, loathing; **Red:** annoyance, anger, rage; **Orange:** interest, anticipation, vigilance.

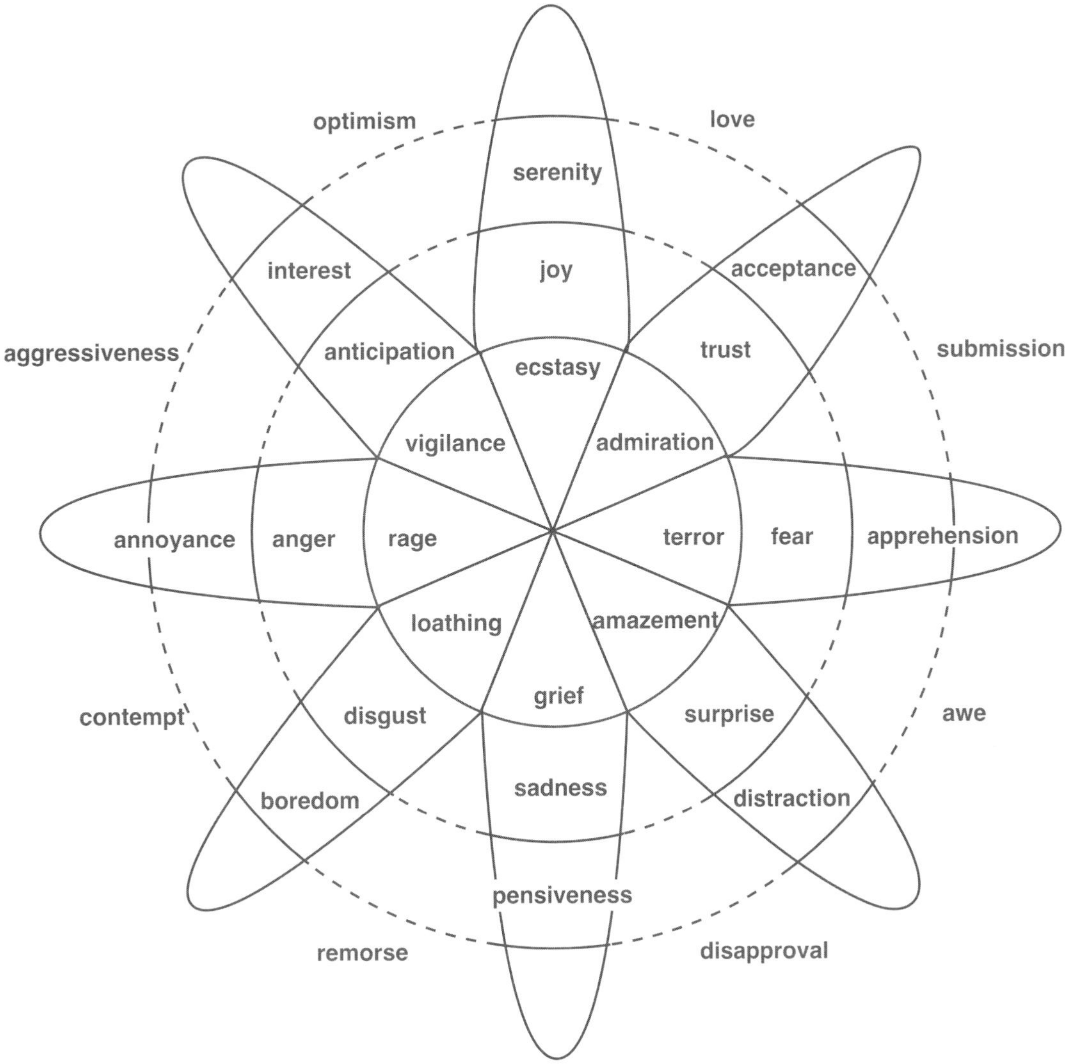

Using the Wheel of Emotions

Coloring the wheel can help tweens and teens get to know it. They're already aware that emotions have opposites, but they'll start noticing connections between the strongest feelings and their subtler cousins.

With practice, they'll be able to use the wheel to recognize, express, and deal with emotions more effectively.

One way to begin using this tool is by playing a game. "Emotion Match" connects words from the Wheel to real-life situations. Start with an event, like a favorite band coming to town. Ask your tween to point to the emotion that matches how they'd feel if that happened.

If they choose "joy," encourage them to explain. For example, they might say, "Come on, Mom! Sunset Potatoes! They're the best!"

Ask how "joy" feels in their body. Is it warm or cool? Do they feel it in their stomach, legs, or arms? Does it make their heart beat faster? Does it make them feel like dancing or crying?

Repeat this game until you both feel comfortable with the chart.

Here are more ideas:

- Watch a movie and pause at powerful moments. Have your tween identify the characters' feelings. Take turns pausing for each other to analyze onscreen emotions.
- Use index cards and colored markers to make emotion cards after each session. Keep the cards to collect a set over time.
- Create a laminated version of the wheel with a spinner. Play a competitive game where the "Emotion Master" spins and gives clues for their partner to guess the emotion. Pantomime and laughter are encouraged.
- Make a "Feeling Weather Report" for each family member on a board or in a journal, using words from the wheel and adding drawings.

- Encourage tweens to read books appropriate for their age group and discuss the characters' feelings using words from the wheel.
- Consider enrolling your tween in a drama or dance group to explore and express emotions through performance. Drama games are great for developing emotional intelligence. You can find many of them online. Here's an example: <https://www.teachingexpertise.com/classroom-ideas/drama-games/>.
- Read favorite poems or short stories. Use the wheel to identify the strongest emotion in each work.
- Visit an art museum and talk about paintings using words from the wheel. Afterward, encourage your teen to create their own artwork expressing similar emotions.

Let's Get Together: A Family Calendar

Families are busy. Each member has many activities outside the home. This adds variety and enriches the family. It connects them with the community and the world beyond. However, people can become too involved with friends, work, and school. They lose touch with loved ones.

Though teens protest, family time is vital for their focus, security, and happiness.

- Begin by having a weekly dinner together. (No phones allowed.) Here are some ideas:
  o Pizza and a salad bar
  o Chili and homemade bread
  o Soup and subs
  o A backyard barbeque
  o A picnic in the park
  o A group cooking project such as Taco Tuesday

- Set up a monthly movie night with popcorn and other healthy snacks. Many local libraries offer DVDs.

- Set aside one Saturday a month for a family outing. Here are some ideas:
  o A sporting event
  o A museum
  o A concert
  o A movie matinee in a theater
  o A beach or pool day
  o A farmer's market
  o An amusement park
  o A hike or bike ride

- Once a year, plan a longer adventure such as a camping trip. Involve your teen in:
  o Mapping out the drive
  o Calculating the budget
  o Requesting brochures
  o Researching points of interest
  o Learning about plants and wildlife

- Visit relatives and invite your teen to record family stories.

- Maintain a communal calendar to coordinate schedules and special events.
  o Mark family dinner nights, movie nights, outings, and trips.
  o Encourage each family member to add their lessons, appointments, and sports.

Name: ___________________________   Date: ___________________________

Family Activity Brainstormer

Directions: Fill this out before the scheduled planning meeting.

Things I'd like to do with the family for our weekly activity day:

1. ____
2. ____
3. ____
4. ____
5. ____
6. ____
7. ____
8. ____
9. ____
10. ____

Places I'd like to go on our annual vacation: (Parents will make the final decision.)

1. ____
2. ____
3. ____
4. ____
5. ____

Movies I'd like to see on Family Movie Night:

1. ____
2. ____
3. ____
4. ____
5. ____
6. ____
7. ____
8. ____

Electronics Use Contract

I, ____, agree to the following:

Responsibility for Equipment: I understand that the phone and computer I use are my parents' property, and I promise to take care of them.

Time Limits: I agree to follow the time limits my parents set for phone and computer use.

Homework First: I understand that I must complete all of my homework and any required study tasks before using the phone or computer for anything else.

Safe and Appropriate Use: I agree to use the phone and computer safely. I will not share personal information online or bully other users. I understand what inappropriate content is and I agree not to access it.

Mealtime and Bedtime: I will not use the phone during meals, and I will sign off the computer and put down the phone at least one hour before bed.

Parental Control Settings: I understand that my parents have activated parental control settings. They have explained that, for my safety, they reserve the right to monitor my use of the phone and computer.

I understand these guidelines and promise to follow them. I also understand that my parents may take away my phone and computer privileges if I do not observe these conditions.

Teen's Signature ____

Parent(s) Signature(s): ____

Date: _______________________________

Super Focus: *Okay, good luck getting your teen to sign this, but it does give you some things to keep in mind. No matter what your middle schooler says, YOU are in charge.*

Sample School Day Schedule

If you home-school, create a similar chart. Use times that are convenient for you. Once established, stick to the schedule and be consistent. Notice that in this example, math and language arts come first. Science and social studies are also in the morning. It is a good idea to take care of hard subjects when students are fresh.

If your teen is enrolled in an online school, substitute that program's times.

Traditional in-person school students should plug in their current class schedules. (It's a good idea to have each room number and teacher's name on file at home.)

Morning:
7:00–7:30 A.M.: (Set an alarm) Wake up. Morning hygiene.

> ***Super Focus:*** *Gather materials including anything that is due. Check the daily planner for in-person or online meetings and assignments.*

7:30–8:00 A.M.: Eat breakfast. (If attending in-person school, allow commuting time.)

Class Schedule

> ***Super Focus:*** *In addition to the 15-minute morning recess, all classes should include a brief stand and stretch break every 20 minutes. Set a timer. This is especially important for students with focus challenges. (See Part II of this book for suggestions.)*

8:00–9:00 A.M.: Math
9:00–10:00 A.M.: Language Arts (Literature and Writing)
10:00–10:15 A.M.: Break
10:15–11:15 A.M.: Science
11:15–12:15 P.M.: Social Studies: History, Civics, Geography
12:15–1:00 P.M.: Lunch

> ***Super Focus:*** *Include lean protein and healthy carbohydrates such as fruit.*

1:00–2:00 P.M.: Foreign Language, Health, Technology, or Other Requirement
2:00–2:30 P.M.: Physical Education (Homeschoolers—a walk or bike ride counts.)
2:30–3:00 P.M.: Art, Music, Drama, Shop, or Other Elective

After School:
3:00–4:00 P.M.: Homework/study time for all subjects
4:00–5:30 P.M.: Chores, outdoor exercise, time with friends, lessons, or sports

Evening:
5:30–6:00 P.M.: Dinner and clean-up
6:00–8:00 P.M.: Hobbies, music practice, family activities, or electronics time
8:00–9:00 P.M.: Electronics off, reading, journaling, nightly hygiene routine

> ***Super Focus:*** *Set out clothes and assemble materials for the next day.*

9:00 P.M.: Bed.

Rewards and Penalties: Brainstormer

Sit down at the kitchen table with your middle schooler on a day when things are going well. Take out some paper and colored markers. Explain that it's time to brainstorm some rewards for positive behavior and penalties for times when guidelines are not followed.

Start the session with rewards. Have your teen choose their favorite-colored marker and list everything they consider a reward. You do the same.

When your teen seems to be finished, trade lists. Share a laugh about the ones that are impossible, admire the ones that are creative, and transfer the most practical ideas to another page. Change marker colors. Repeat the process for penalties.

Every family is different, so it's best to come up with your own ideas. However, if you are stuck, here are some standard suggestions to get you started:

Rewards:

- extra screen time
- staying up late on Saturday night
- extra time with friends
- a movie at the theater
- a pro baseball, football, or basketball game
- shooting hoops or playing catch with Dad/Mom
- a day out shopping and lunch with Dad/Mom
- a favorite snack or dessert

Penalties:
- apologies and amends
- replacing lost or broken property

For limited periods such as a day or a week:

- no recreational screen time
- no video games
- no phone privileges
- grounding (no time with friends outside of school)
- extra chores

End this collaborative session with one of the suggested rewards for a job well done (and a hug if your teen will allow it). Keep the resulting lists in a safe place.

> **Super Focus:** Use rewards as often as possible. With penalties, above all, be consistent.

Creating a Study Space

Studying is brain work. It requires a quiet, uncluttered environment. This is especially true for students who have trouble concentrating.

- Choose a room for the study space.

- Help your middle schooler create a scale drawing. (This is a math skill.) Include existing furniture, windows, and doors. If furniture must be moved, cut scale shapes from colored construction paper. Try the pieces in various positions before completing the drawing.

- Invite your teen to search online for study nook ideas. Help the student make an inventory of what you already own. Make a list of missing essentials.

- With your middle schooler, create a budget. Stretching available dollars can be fun. Take your tween with you to garage sales and discount stores. Make it a challenge.

- So, your plan is complete. Supplies have been gathered. It's time to assemble a team to help with physical labor such as furniture moving or painting. Workers can either be hired or recruited from friends and relatives.

- If using volunteers, have your middle schooler make phone calls and write thank-you notes. If you hire professionals such as painters or electricians, encourage your teen to ask them about their jobs.

> **Super Focus:** *This is not the only way to set up a study space. It would be easier to do everything yourself but consider the applied academic skills included in this project. Studies have shown that students focus better when they see a purpose for what they are learning.*

Study Space Requirements
- Desk or table
- Chair
- Desk lamp (needs an electrical outlet)
- Bookshelf or bookcase
- Paper
- Pencils and pens
- Inbox and outbox
- If possible: A computer or tablet and a printer, which can be shared. (Needs an outlet with power strip surge protector.)

Music Magic: 60 Beats Per Minute for Concentration

Quiet is important for studying, but it isn't always possible. This is especially true if you live near a highway or there are young children in the house.

Headphones can work to block out noise. Instrumental music helps some students concentrate. The best pieces for focus have a tempo of about 60 beats per minute. This pace matches the resting heartbeat.

Here are some examples. You have probably heard at least one of them. They help you relax without putting you to sleep.

"Moonlight Sonata" by Ludwig van Beethoven (first movement)
"Air" from *Orchestral Suite No. 3 in D Major* by Johann Sebastian Bach
"Piano Concerto No. 21" by Wolfgang Amadeus Mozart (second movement)
"Clair de Lune" by Claude Debussy
"Meditation" from *Thaïs* by Jules Massenet
"Für Elise" by Ludwig van Beethoven
"Adagio in G Minor" by Tomaso Albinoni
"Canon in D" by Johann Pachelbel

Many current songs are performed at this tempo, but most have vocals. Lyrics can be distracting. To find appropriate popular music, search streaming services for study or reading playlists. If you don't have Internet access or a music streaming service, stick with pieces like the ones above.

In the 90s, there was a popular theory called The Mozart Effect. It claimed that listening to Baroque music made children smarter. Later research disproved the idea, but even if they don't turn kids into geniuses, instrumental works can block distracting sounds and help some middle schoolers focus. Works from the Baroque period are usually available on CDs through local public libraries. Sometimes, they turn up at garage sales or in second-hand shops.

> ***Super Focus:*** *Music helps some people calm down and think more clearly. Unfortunately, it bothers others. Such students work best in silence. Listen to your teen. Understand and support different learning styles. (White noise can also be used to block out distractions.)*

The Pomodoro Technique:
5-Minute, 10-Minute, and 20-Minute Tasks

The Pomodoro Technique helps people work efficiently.

- Users of this system break tasks into short sessions called "Pomodoros." Each 25-minute work period is followed by a five-minute break.
- This method can help middle school students who struggle with focus. Big projects seem less scary when divided into small chunks.
- Introduce the Pomodoro technique to your middle schooler.
  - o Explain the method and its benefits.
  - o Show how to break a current assignment into parts.
  - o Provide a kitchen timer to pace work sessions and breaks.
- With your teen, list some five-minute break activities, some ten-minute tasks, and some twenty-minute projects.
  - o Everyone works at a different speed, so getting it right may take practice.
  - o Here are some examples to get you started:

5-Minute Break Ideas:
- Straighten up your desk.
- Grab a sandwich.
- Play with the dog.
- Dance to a favorite song.

10-Minute Tasks:
- Read a textbook page and summarize the main ideas.
- Brainstorm topics for a class project or a story.
- Practice a piano piece.
- Review class notes and highlight or circle important points.
- Solve a math problem or two. Review any steps, rules, or formulas.

20-Minute Tasks:
- Read a history chapter and take notes.
- Use a search engine to gather information for a report.
- Draft an outline for an essay.
- Review class and reading notes for a history test.
- Create a chart or diagram using online software.
- Work on a model for science class.

Super Focus: *A surprising number of study tasks can be completed in five minutes or less. Once teens are used to this system, they may finish brief assignments either at school or as soon as they get home. This satisfying strategy helps curb procrastination.*

Parent-Teacher Communication

Effective communication with your child's teacher is very important. If you have a question, request, or concern, it can be helpful to contact the teacher directly. Use this sample form to set up a time and method for addressing the concern.

To: (Teacher's Name) _______________________________________

Date: _______________________

Attention Requested (circle one) Immediately / This Week / At Your Earliest Convenience

Student's Name: _______________________________________

Grade: _____________ Subject/Class: _____________________ Period: ___________

Question, Request, or Concern:

____

____

____

____

____

____

____

Parent's Name: _______________________________________

Phone Number: _____________________ Email: _____________________

Preferred Method of Communication: (circle one) Phone / Email / In-Person Meeting

Best time to call: (circle one) Before School / After School / Evening / Other: _______________

ADD, ADHD, or Other Special Needs

Parenting a teen with ADHD is never easy, but here are some things to try:

- Research ADHD. Find out how your teen experiences the world. This understanding can help you and other family members provide more effective support.

- Establish a regular routine. Consistency and predictability help ADHD teens feel less confused. Meals, homework, bedtime, and even breaks should be scheduled.

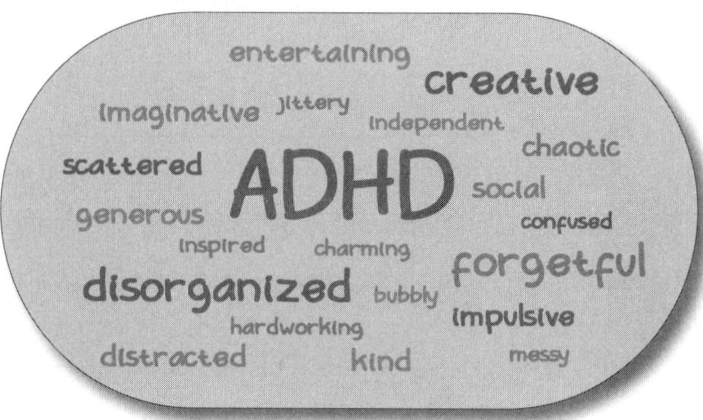

- Teens with ADHD have trouble sorting out what's important from what isn't. Give directions in clear simple steps. Leave out unnecessary details and explanations.

- Sit down together and set a few simple goals. When a target is reached, take time to celebrate. There's nothing like success to build confidence and increase motivation.

- Recognize positive behavior. Praise your middle schooler for being kind, stopping to think before reacting, remembering materials, and completing tasks on time.

- When imposing penalties, remain calm and, above all, be consistent. This is important for all kids, but especially those with ADD or ADHD.

- Limit video games and other electronics as much as possible. Some families may need to eliminate them. Observe their effect on your teen and act accordingly. A log of your teen's use of such devices and their behavior can help you decide.

- Keep furnishings and décor simple. Eliminate clutter. Create a place to slow down and breathe.

- You won't be able to do all this yourself. Keep a clear line of communication open with your partner as well as your child's doctor, therapist, and school counselor. You may need to keep in touch with teachers daily.

- Consider joining an organization or online group for parents of children with ADD or ADHD. Such alliances offer valuable support.

> **Super Focus:** *Each teen with ADHD is unique. What works for one may not help another. Your child has tremendous energy and is very sensitive. These attributes may lead to success, but they are also challenges.*

Parent Resources: Books, Websites, and Organizations

Books:

ADHD: What Every Parent Needs to Know by Michael I. Reiff

Driven to Distraction: Recognizing and Coping with Attention Deficit Disorder by Edward M. Hallowell, M.D. and John J. Ratey, M.D.

Smart but Scattered: The Revolutionary "Executive Skills" Approach to Helping Kids Reach Their Potential by Peg Dawson and Richard Guare

Taking Charge of ADHD: The Complete, Authoritative Guide for Parents by Russell A. Barkley

The ADHD Workbook for Kids: Helping Children Gain Self-Confidence, Social Skills, and Self-Control by Lawrence E. Shapiro

Articles:

"Helping Your Child with ADHD Succeed in School" by Understood.org

"Middle School and ADHD: Tips for Parents" by ADDitude Magazine

"ADHD in Middle School: What Parents Should Know" by Child Mind Institute

"Managing ADHD in Middle School" by CHADD (Children and Adults with Attention-Deficit/Hyperactivity Disorder)

Websites:

ADDitude Magazine <www.additudemag.com>

American Academy of Child and Adolescent Psychiatry <https://www.aacap.org/AACAP/Families_Youth/Resource_Centers/AACAP/Families_and_Youth/Resource_Centers/ADHD_Resource_Center/Home.aspx>

CHADD (Children and Adults with Attention-Deficit/Hyperactivity Disorder) <www.chadd.org>

Resources for ADHD (Web MD) <https://www.webmd.com/add-adhd/childhood-adhd/adhd-resources>

Understood.org <www.understood.org>

Organizations:

CHADD (Children and Adults with Attention-Deficit/Hyperactivity Disorder)

National Resource Center on ADHD

The Attention Deficit Disorder Association (ADDA)

Part II: Focus Basics for Educators

Middle school can be overwhelming. During these years, students leave childhood and move toward young adulthood. Common challenges they face include:

- social and emotional adjustment
- complex academic material
- accountability for supplies
- responsibility for time management
- relationships with multiple teachers
- adaptation to a larger school

It's not surprising that many middle schoolers struggle with focus. Even the most diligent sometimes forget materials and daydream during presentations.

Whatever the subject matter, tweens need extra guidance to focus effectively. Fortunately, there are many tools to help. Part II of *Focus for Success* will explore tested ways to help students engage fully in class.

These strategies include:

- setting clear expectations and goals
- creating a structured learning environment
- using positive reinforcement
- maintaining partnerships with parents and other teachers
- incorporating mindfulness techniques
- establishing a standard active response (e.g., thumbs up)
- incorporating movement into every class session
- designing directed social interactions such as group projects or book clubs
- teaching active listening, including notetaking
- delivering instructions in clear, sequential steps
- building motivation with real-world applications of course material

At the end of this section, you will find a list of resources. These articles, books, websites, and organizations offer valuable additional information and support. For example, one site listed on the Part II resource page allows you to make puzzles for classroom use. Puzzles are great for teaching and reviewing important math, science, social studies, art, and music vocabulary.

You can access most of these references online or through your local public library. You may also find useful ideas in other parts of this book. Check the Table of Contents for possibilities. Some pages in the section for parents may be useful for teachers too. Mandalas and mazes in the student section can serve as brain breaks in class.

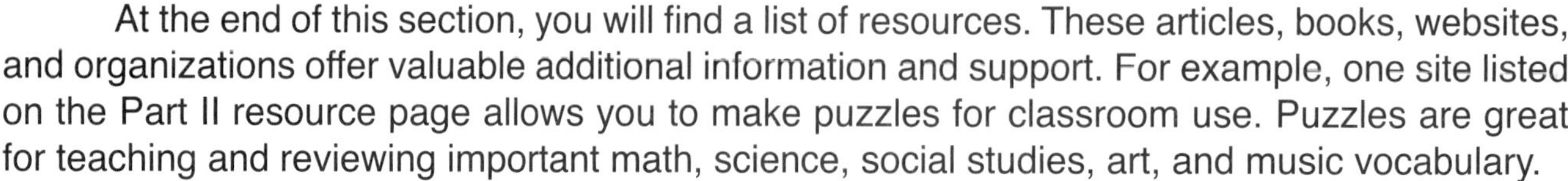

The Value of Predictability: A Sample Schedule

So much of life is unpredictable for middle schoolers. Knowing what to expect in class can help. Parents also appreciate knowing what is being covered and when to expect homework.

Here's a sample weekly plan to get you started. Introduce your own schedule at Back-to-School Night. Continue sharing it using your school's preferred communication path.

Subject: ____

Monday

Lesson: Introduction to ____

Three important things: ____

Class discussion: ____

Homework: Read and take notes on pages _______________________________________

Tuesday

Lesson: ____

Three important things: ____

Group activity: ____

Homework: Complete the worksheet: ____

Wednesday

Lesson: ____

Three important things: ____

Class debate: ____

Homework: Write a paragraph about: ____

Thursday

Lesson: ____

Class activity: ____

Review of important things: ____

Homework: Study for the quiz.

Friday

Lesson: ____

Quiz and class activity.

Homework: Ongoing project.

Overcoming Student Anxiety: A Sample Guided Visualization Script

If you have never experienced guided visualization, there are many to try online. They are a great way to relax. Use something like this for a mid-lesson break or on days when the wind is wild and so are the students.

Practice reading this script aloud before sharing it. Feel free to adapt the language to suit your group and your personality. Your presentation should be unhurried and sound natural. The forest is a classic setting, but if you don't like it, write one for your favorite place.

Say:

Get comfortable. Close your eyes and take a deep breath through your nose. Fill your lungs with air. Hold it. Now, slowly breathe out, feeling all your muscles relax.

Imagine you are in the mountains at the edge of a beautiful evergreen forest. A soft breeze whispers through the trees. Squirrels chatter and birds sing in the branches overhead. As you enter the woods, a carpet of pine needles cushions your steps.

A well-worn trail leads down a hill, deeper into the shadows. As you walk along, the trees start getting taller. The air is cool and pine-scented. Sunlight filters through branches high above. Dappled shade dances across the path. Feathery ferns curl and delicate wildflowers bloom on either side. You spot a doe and her fawn watching you from behind some bushes. They aren't afraid. You take a deep breath. The air filling your lungs is fresh and sweet.

Ahead, beyond the trees, there's a spot of golden sunlight. It is a clearing. As you get closer, there's the unmistakable sound of water playing over rocks. You love creeks, and it sounds so inviting. When you reach the meadow, the warm sun feels so good on your face. You spot the little stream right away. Its clear water sparkles. You settle down on the grassy bank.

You take off your shoes and socks and feel the cool water flow between your toes. You close your eyes and take a deep breath in, filling your lungs with fresh, cool air. As you exhale, your worries leave your body. They turn into colorful, silly-looking bugs, almost like cartoons, lazily sunning themselves in the grass.

A little folded paper boat floats down the stream toward you. When it comes close, you reach out and grab it. You carefully place the bugs in the boat. They seem happy there, ready for a new adventure. You put the boat back into the water. It floats downstream, carrying your worries away.

You sit by the stream a little longer, enjoying the peaceful meadow and the warm sun. You take a deep breath in and slowly exhale, feeling completely calm. When you are ready, open your eyes and notice how you feel. Remember, you can come back any time and let the cool stream carry your worries away.

The Pomodoro Technique for Teachers: A Focus-Friendly Sample Lesson

Subject: Language Arts
Grade Level: Middle School (7th grade)
Duration: 60 minutes
Objective: Students will draft a short story using the *Pomodoro Technique*.
Materials:

    A writing prompt   Timer or stopwatch

Procedure:

- **Introduction (5 minutes)**
  - Explain that students will be drafting a short-short story using the *Pomodoro Technique*, a method many people, including writers, use to focus.
- **Present or review these four key steps of the Pomodoro Technique: (5–10 minutes)**
  - Step 1: Set a timer (for 15–25 minutes).
  - Step 2: Work until the timer sounds.
  - Step 3: Take a short break.
  - Step 4: Repeat steps 1–3.

Begin the Writing Process

- **Pomodoro 1: Story planning (10 minutes)**
  - Provide a simple story starter. Encourage students to spend the first Pomodoro (time chunk) listing several possible goals, settings, obstacles, and resolutions.
  - Set the timer.
  - Instruct students to brainstorm until the timer dings.
- **Break: Lead the class in a quick movement activity such as Simon Says.**
- **Pomodoro 2: Story outlining (15 minutes)**
  - Students will use the second Pomodoro to outline their stories.
  - Set the timer for 15 minutes.
  - Advise them to include one main character, a goal, at least one obstacle, and a resolution in their outlines. (This is practice. It can be silly.)
- **Break: Lead students in a brief stand-up, sit-down activity.**
- **Pomodoro 3: Writing a rough draft (15 minutes)**
  - After the break, set your timer and challenge the students to write drafts of their stories. Tell them to write fast without worrying about mistakes. Remind them they can change anything or everything later.

> ***Super Focus:*** *Students with ADD may struggle with this loose approach. Work with them individually during each Pomodoro. They find a wide array of possibilities confusing. Offer them specific suggestions.*

Conclusion: Review the key steps of the Pomodoro Technique.
Extension:

- Encourage students to use the Pomodoro Technique at home when creating a final draft of this story.
- Explain that after three or four 15- or 20-minute Pomodoros, users of this system take a 20-minute break.

The Cornell Method of Note Taking: A Graphic Organizer

Encouraged by some colleges and universities, this way of taking notes helps many students concentrate on what's important.

Students jot down notes on the main ideas in the right-hand column as they listen. Then after the class, they write the most important points, questions, or comments, in a few words, on the left side in the cues section. At the end of the note-taking session, they summarize the session's content in a sentence or two. This is the overall "What did I learn?" section.

A good way to practice note taking is with a short, approved instructional film.

CUES/QUESTIONS	NOTES/MAIN IDEAS

SUMMARY

Super Focus: For extra practice, students can take notes on a YouTube or Vimeo documentary. These films are well-organized and repeatable. (Please do not insist on this form beyond an introductory lesson or two. It is only one way of taking notes. Some students prefer an informal outline or a graphic technique.)

Snap, Clap, or Stand: A Peer-to-Peer Brainstormer for ASR

In the first part of a lesson, it's common to review previously covered information. If you don't already, try asking questions that can be answered in one of two or three physical ways (think Simon Says moves). This is called **active student responding (ASR)**.

For example, in 6th-grade science, you might say, "If gneiss is an igneous rock, put your hands on your head, if it's a metamorphic rock, put your hands on your shoulders, and if it's a sedimentary rock, fold your arms. Show me now!" You'll be able to see right away if the class has the idea. If you need to reteach, take care of it.

You can also use this technique to hold the group's attention as you present new material. Ask for opinions about which step to take next in a math word problem. Say something like, "Stand up and stay standing if you think we should multiply. Stand up and sit back down if you think we should divide."

Many middle school teachers have standard responses. For example, "Nod if you understand. Shake your head if you don't, and I'll explain again." When a student volunteers an answer, say "Thumbs up if you agree. Thumbs down if you disagree." All should be prepared to explain their responses. Such techniques keep everyone involved.

You and other teachers at your school probably have some great engagement tricks. Try having a quick get-together at school or online to share ideas. Before the meeting, make a list of group response techniques that work in your classroom. Be prepared to take notes, because one idea can trigger more.

The teachers you meet with don't have to share your subject or grade. Keep an open mind. Some surprising things are effective.

Here are some common strategies to try:

- **Choral response:** The teacher starts a statement or asks a question, and the class responds aloud together on an agreed signal such as a bell, a clicker, or "Say it now!"

- **Whiteboard tablet response:** After a short writing period, all students hold up tablets with their answers.

- **Preprinted card response:** On a spoken cue or a bell, students hold up a preprinted card saying "True," "False," "Agree," "Disagree," or other relevant responses.

- **Clickers:** Click if you agree.

> **Super Focus:** For more information, check out this great site or plug the phrase "Active Student Responding" into your favorite search engine.
> <https://www.winginstitute.org/instructional-delivery-student-respond>

Name: _______________________________

Date: _______________________________

Social Learning: A Student Team Graphic Organizer

Title: _______________________________

Class: _________________ **Period:** _________ **Teacher:** _________________

Main ideas to be covered: ____

____

Draft due: _________________ **Final project due:** _________________

Format of presentation: (e.g. video, essay, display, etc.) _________________

Team Members	Responsibilities	Collecting Information	Writing/ Presenting

Incorporating Movement: Pool Noodle Drumming and Other Happy Insanity

Too much sitting takes a toll on any tween's ability to focus. Breaking up the class for short group activities can help. For example, in social studies, after a brief review of issues, students might take sides in a debate. Suppose the question is: *Should Homework be Eliminated?* After five minutes of jotting down their most important arguments, students in favor move to one side of the room, and those opposed move to the other. They share points they want to emphasize with each other before presenting them. Getting up and walking across the room creates a mini brain break. If participants stand to present their points of argument, that's a bonus. Here are more ideas:

- The Cornell University Center for Teaching Innovation offers social learning activities. Many naturally involve moving around. Find them on this site: <https://teaching.cornell.edu/resource/examples-collaborative-learning-or-group-work-activities> or plug the keywords *middle school collaborative learning* into any search engine.
- The site *Minds in Bloom* offers a collection of 20 mini-games that take just three minutes and get the blood flowing. One idea shared there is the *Difficult Physical Task*. Challenge students to touch their toes without bending their knees, stand on one foot without touching anything, or do a standing yoga pose. *Minds in Bloom* is here: <https://minds-in-bloom.com/20-three-minute-brain-breaks>. To find other collections, use the keywords *middle school brain breaks.*
- If you want something simple, but fun, try a quick round of Simon Says, invite students to dance in place to an energetic popular song, or just let them wander around the room for two or three minutes and visit with friends. Be sure to have a sign, such as a raised hand they copy, signaling it's time for work to resume.
- Speaking of popular songs, check out YouTube's pool noodle desk drumming videos. These can be done in the classroom or at home. They are great fun and provide a surprising workout in a very short time. You will need to purchase and cut up some pool noodles. (They're cheap and last a long time.) You will also need internet access or some kind of audio player. The master of these wonderfully silly workouts is Kent Hamilton. Look for his videos on YouTube. Here's one for starters. <https://youtu.be/xVIXnuGs7hg>. 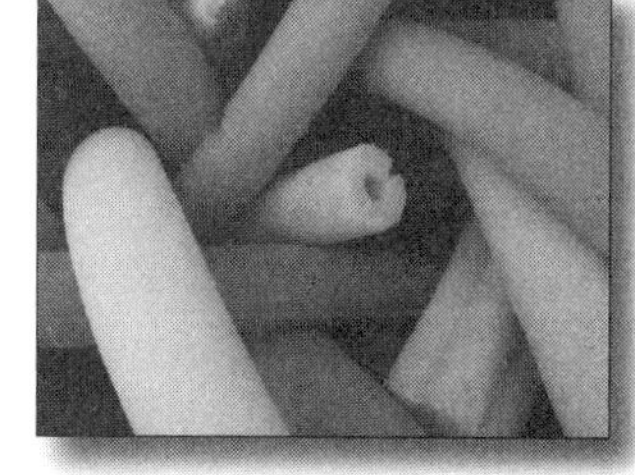
- Active breaks are important, but brain breaks can be quiet too. If students take three minutes to close their eyes and imagine a peaceful place, it can refresh their minds and improve their focus for the rest of the period. World geography, for example, could provide a wonderful opportunity to mentally visit a beach in France. In Language Arts, try playing recordings of poets reading their work. The *Poetry Archive* offers an amazing collection. Here's Elizabeth Bishop. <https://poetryarchive.org/poet/elizabeth-bishop/>
- Paper challenges such as Sudoku, crosswords, or adult coloring pages also provide relaxing breaks. Sometimes puzzles or coloring activities can be built into a lesson. Map coloring is one good example. A scientific diagram is another. Vocabulary lists in any subject lend themselves to crosswords. Several free websites allow users to create puzzles for home or classroom use.

Tips for Starting a Book Club: Hints From Amy Armstrong, Therapeutic Book Club Organizer

Book clubs are popular with adults for good reasons. They offer a chance to share a new, ongoing experience. They are structured. With an appropriate self-help book, a club can improve such skills as making friends, time management, or self-care. With a novel, it can be a starting place for sharing feelings and experiences. Here are some tips for organizing a middle school book club:

Choosing a good book for the group.
- Is it readily available in a variety of formats, and is it available at the library? Some people need to be able to read books electronically or listen to audio, so it helps to pick something that is accessible to everyone.
- While it's tempting to choose something that is new and "buzzworthy," a book that has been out for a while is more likely to have resources available like a reader's guide from the author or publisher and other support materials. While these aren't essential, they can be helpful in enhancing the experience for your group members when you're just starting out.
- Consider broad appeal for the people you most want to invite to the group. While book clubs can be a good learning opportunity for everyone, it's important to choose something that will make group members feel welcome and create a positive group experience. "Forcing" a sticky issue on others can backfire if they aren't ready to talk about it.

Prepare.
- Read the book before you start the group and review important chapters before the meeting.
- Highlight and flag passages that resonate with you and make notes.
- Prepare discussion questions.
- Do some research and find articles, films, and other materials that are related to the book to share with group members.

Be a good host.
- Show up to every meeting.
- Greet everyone.
- Make sure you have refreshments and a welcoming environment if you're meeting in person.
- Send out reminders for the meeting along with some prepared questions.
- Send a follow-up message after the meeting with a summary of key points discussed and any supplemental resources that might be helpful.
- Listen to what other group members share. Show you're listening by summarizing what they've said and encouraging others to ask follow-up questions or share their thoughts on any points they shared.
- Expect that some members will talk more, and others will talk less. Affirm from the start that's okay, but also set the norm and expectation that if someone is dominating the conversation, you would like other people to have the opportunity to share.
- Be gracious about the fact that not everyone will be able to finish all the reading before the meeting, and that's okay.

Name: ___________________　　Date: ___________________

Real-World Applications: A Brainstormer for Students

What is the biggest problem in the world?

____

____

____

Why is that problem important?

____

____

____

____

____

Who could solve that problem?

____

____

How could subjects you are studying right now help solve the problem?

____

____

Name other important world problems.

____

____

____

What would you do if a magician gave you a ring that allowed you to accomplish anything during your life? How would the skills you are learning now help you?

____

____

____

____

Classroom Teacher Resources: Books, Websites, and Organizations

Books:

Executive Function in the Classroom: Practical Strategies for Improving Performance and Enhancing Skills for All Students by Christopher Kaufman

Lost at School: Why Our Kids with Behavioral Challenges Are Falling Through the Cracks and How We Can Help Them by Ross W. Greene

Teach Like a Champion: 49 Techniques that Put Students on the Path to College by Doug Lemov

Teaching with Love and Logic: Taking Control of the Classroom by Charles Fay and David Funk

The Skillful Teacher: Building Your Teaching Skills by Jon Saphier

Articles:

"Fostering Student Engagement and Active Learning in the Classroom" by Michael S. Prince *(Journal of Engineering Education)*

"Improving Middle School Students' Attention and Engagement" by Amy L. Reschly and Sandra L. Christenson *(Preventing School Failure: Alternative Education for Children and Youth)*

"Increasing Student Engagement and Attention: The Importance of High-Quality Instruction" by Robert H. Tai and Helen H. S. Tai *(Journal of Science Education and Technology)*

"Promoting Attention and Self-Regulation for Children with Learning Challenges" by Lynn Meltzer *(Zero to Three Journal)*

"Strategies for Increasing Student Engagement and Active Learning in the Classroom" by John R. Clayton and Carol H. Zepke *(Research in Higher Education Journal)*

Websites:

Edutopia <www.edutopia.org>: Provides resources on educational topics, including strategies to improve student focus.

Internet4Classrooms <https://www.internet4classrooms.com/links_grades_kindergarten_12/game_puzzle_makers_teacher_tools.htm> : Game and puzzle makers

Teach Thought <www.teachthought.com>: Offers articles and blog posts related to teaching techniques and classroom management strategies.

Responsive Classroom <www.responsiveclassroom.org>: Provides resources to create a classroom environment that fosters focus.

National Association of School Psychologists <www.nasponline.org>: Features helpful articles on student behavior, including attention and focus.

Teach Starter <www.teachstarter.com>: Offers ways to engage students and improve their focus during lessons.

Name: Date:

Part III: A Focus Workbook for Students

Relax With Coloring

Directions: Coloring can be a relaxing way to improve focus. Color this mandala. Use any colors but stay inside the lines. Some people say it isn't creative to color this way, but it has a different purpose. You aren't creating an original work of art. It is more like meditating. It takes concentration and pulls your mind away from your problems.

For more of a challenge, discover the symmetry in this design and emphasize it with the colors you choose.

Name:　　　　　　　　　　　　　　　　　　　Date:

What Do I Love? A Brainstormer

　　　Everybody's different. It's important to know what you love to do. Give this some thought. You can do lots of versions of this exercise, and you will probably change your mind as weeks and months go by. This worksheet is a starting place.

Directions: Fill in the shapes with things that you love to do. Add drawings. Later, grab a sheet of poster paper and your favorite markers to add more favs. Post it in your room for inspiration.

Name:

Date:

The Magic Wand: A Journal Prompt

Directions: You have the power to change your life. What do you change? What do you gain? What do you miss? Write about it on the lines below.

Super Focus: *What do you like about yourself and the way your life is right now? Write a paragraph or two in your journal.*

Name:

Date:

Find the Feelings: An Emotion Word Search

Directions: Find and circle the feelings words in the word search puzzle. Answers may be printed forward or backward, horizontally, vertically, or diagonally.

Amazed
Amused
Anger
Anticipation
Anxious
Aware
Awe
Caution
Cautious
Comfortable
Contentment
Critical
Depressed
Disgust
Disinterest
Dismissive
Distracted
Ecstatic
Elation
Excited
Fear
Frustrated
Grief
Happiness
Hatred
Hopeful
Hurt
Impatient
Insulted
Jealous
Joy

```
C R O L L W N X Q D G Y M T F Q Z F D
I R F Y H O U D E T C A R T S I D N E
T J S K I X J T G S G X J W S K Y Z S
A W A T S R A D S U I U O B O B Y I U
T T U N K R D Z E G W L Y E H E W I M
S A C D T S P F L S V E L A T I O N A
C U A S E I U A Y I S U A W A R E S D
E V U T A R C O V D F E I L B N G U E
N R T Q N I T I L E F M R A L R P L Z
F N I B X H Y A P A P A N P I N D T A
K B O L I A A O H A E F I E E U G E M
K W U B O P H D T F T J F M H D B D A
D P S M U P C I R C G I N U W G W I C
Q K Q R S I E T C O M F O R T A B L E
N H E D A N P R C O N T E N T M E N T
E X C I T E D U T O H E W A O T Y P Q
U C F Z V S Y H T S E R E T N I S I D
D I S M I S S I V E C R I T I C A L H
G R E G N A F I E U K H Z I E S E S C
```

Super Focus: *Choose one of these feeling words. Write about a time when you or a friend felt that way. Draw a picture to go with the story, or create a doodle expressing that feeling.*

Name: ___________________   Date: ___________________

My Private Brain Dump: A Journal Prompt

Directions: When you are frustrated, sad, or disappointed, dump your feelings on a page like this. You can add pictures from magazines, sketches, or doodles if you want. Keep it or tear it into little bits. It's up to you.

Name:

Date:

Distracto Destructo: A Dot-to-Dot Puzzle and Graphic Story Prompt

Directions: Connect the dots to reveal what's trashing Concentration City. Then, in your journal, or on another paper, draw your own distraction monster. Give it a name. Create a story or comic about how you, as a superhero, tame it or destroy it.

Name: ___________________________   Date: ___________________________

Distraction-Busters: A Word Search

Directions: Find and circle the words related to distraction-busting in the word search puzzle. Answers may be printed forward or backward, horizontally, vertically, or diagonally.

Awareness
Blocks
Breaks
Breathe
Choose
Clutter
Concentration
Differences
Distraction
Electronics
Energy
Focus
Headphones
Hydration
Individual
Instrumental
Lighting
Mindful
Movement
Music
Relaxation
Slow
Snacks
Space
Supplies

```
S E C N E R E F F I D P L S J Q U
E S O O H C I S U M R F U W F S U
F R E L A X A T I O N Z F M C Q A
Y G R E N E Z P B H Q Q D I Q A A
L I G H T I N G S R P W N S L O W
R F J C L U T T E R E O I L D L A
N I A W L E S U N G R A M H M A R
O P N S D L D K E T Y P T W O T E
I X O U K B L O C K S Y C H V N N
T O I P J F E E C A G J T D E E E
C N T P Y H L H J F N U A N M M S
A M A L R E F N O S T S I A E U S
R A R I W G Y C B V F F U U N R X
T J D E L A U D I V I D N I T T G
S N Y S U S I D L K B R E A K S P
I Y H S E N O H P D A E H U V N J
D C O N C E N T R A T I O N A I W
```

Write about it: Choose three words that describe things that help you focus. Write a paragraph, a letter, or a blog post using those words to help a friend who's having trouble finishing their schoolwork. Continue on your own paper if needed.

____

____

____

____

____

Name: Date:

Brain Foods: A Crossword Puzzle

Directions: Complete the crossword puzzle with foods that are good for brain function and concentration. The number in parentheses indicates how many letters are in the word.

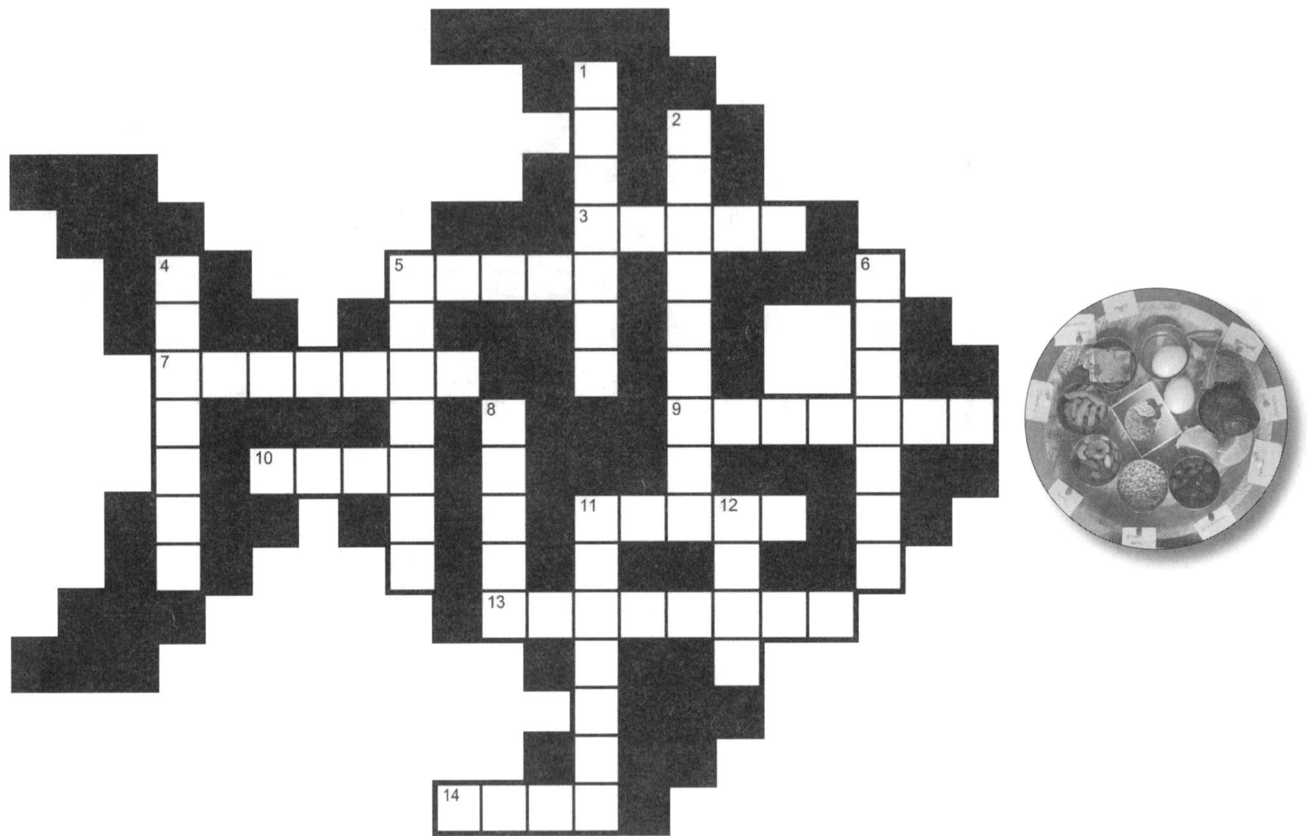

Across

3. A whole-grain form of rice (5)
5. Mac and cheese is healthier if this is whole grain. (5)
7. A hot whole-grain cereal (7)
9. Sweet nuts usually sliced or slivered (7)
10. A protein-rich soybean curd (4)
11. Red power vegetable, best roasted (5)
13. Tiny fish jam-packed with healthy fats (8)
14. Sunny-side-up source of B vitamins (4)

Down

1. Coleslaw's main ingredient (7)
2. Made from cocoa, the dark kind is brain food. (9)
4. Guacamole! (7)
5. Ballpark favorite rich in protein (7)
6. Brain-shaped source of omega-3s in a shell (7)
8. Tasty snacks from sunflowers or pumpkins (5)
11. Red, blue, or black, they're all yummy. (7)
12. A fish that's a sandwich favorite (4)

> **Super Focus:** *Find a recipe online or in a book that uses one or two of the healthy foods in this puzzle. Gather the other ingredients and follow the directions. Write a review of the results. Search online or in the nutrition section of the library to find more healthy foods. Try some of the ones you haven't tasted before.*

Name: Date:

Getting it All Together: A Morning Memo Board Page

Directions: Fill in a memo board like this every night before bed. Check it every morning. A whiteboard or chalkboard is great, but plain paper or a planner is fine. Just put it where you can't miss seeing it. Preparing can save hours of work. Most days, you will just need the materials section and one of the others.

Materials for School:

☐ Backpack   ☐ Forms Signed by Parents

☐ Books   ☐ Lunch and snacks (food, money, or tickets)

☐ Binder   ☐ Water bottle

☐ Tablet   ☐ Other ___________________________

Assignments Due: _________________________________

____

____

Tests or Quizzes: _________________________________

____

Meetings: ____

____

Rehearsals, Lessons, Tutoring, or Sports: ____________

____

____

Appointments: _____________________________________

____

____

Chores: ____

____

Word of the Day: __________________________________

Building a Vision Board: A Collage Craft Project

Making a **Vision Board** is a powerful way to bring dreams to life. It's also fun.

Directions: You will need
- A large sheet of poster board
- Scissors
- Glue
- Colored markers
- Old magazines
- Junk mail and catalogs
- Glitter, sequins, or stickers (optional)

Start by thinking about what you want. For this project, no dream is too wild or too crazy. Don't worry about what other people will think. Don't listen to the little voice in your head that says you aren't deserving. Just have fun imagining your best possible world. Here are a few ideas to get you started:
- Emotions you want to feel more often
- Skills or habits you want to develop
- A career you would like to have
- Sports you would like to play

Go through the magazines and junk mail. Cut out words and pictures that catch your attention. If they don't go with your dream, it's okay. Cut them out anyway.

When you have a pile of cutouts, arrange them on the board in a way that looks good and makes sense to you. If you have too much white space, cut out more pictures. If you have too many items, keep the ones you like best and discard the rest.

Glue the words and pictures down. Then take a break to let the board dry. When you come back, use markers to draw squares or stars around your favorite pictures. Add arrows, doodles, sketches, and glitter or stickers. When your board seems finished, draw a fancy frame around the edges.

Use wall-safe adhesives or tacks to display your vision board in your room. (Ask for help with this, especially if your house or apartment is rented. Some kinds of tape can ruin wall coverings.)

This vision board is yours, and it is right for you right now. Dreams change. It's okay. You can make a new one any time you want to.

If you want to see samples of boards made by others, type "vision board" into a search engine. Hundreds of examples made by people of all ages will appear. There's no wrong way to do this project. Enjoy!

Name: Date:

Sleep for Success: A Crossword Puzzle

Directions: Complete the crossword puzzle with things related to getting a good night's sleep. The number in parentheses indicates how many letters are in the word.

Across

4. Something to avoid after noon (8)
6. A relaxing nighttime activity (7)
8. Special noise that masks distracting sounds (5)
10. Something you do every night to wind down (7)
11. A place just for sleep (3)
12. What to turn off an hour before bed (11)
15. Time for the mind and body to heal (5)
17. A written way to process the day's events (7)
18. A warm one can help you relax (4)
19. If too large or rich, this will keep you awake (4)
20. Has wonderful programs to keep you awake (10)
21. Something to play with family before bed (4)
22. The opposite of noise (5)

Down

1. What will improve with optimum sleep (5)
2. A bedtime schedule that is the same every day improves sleep (10)
3. A relaxing puzzle (6)
5. The light environment that is best for sleep (8)
7. A recorded relaxation script (13)
9. The number of hours of sleep most teens need (4)
11. Something to read with no electronic screen (4)
12. Get this during the day and sleep better at night (8)
13. The best temperature for sleep (4)
14. A drink that contains caffeine (4)
16. A friend-filled distraction to hide until morning (5)
18. The color of light that disrupts sleep (4)

Name: Date:

P is for Perfectionism: A Maze

Perfection seems like a great goal. Who wouldn't want to be perfect? Actually, it is a trap. People who try to get everything right never learn or finish anything. Humans learn by making mistakes.

Directions: Use a pencil to find your way from the top of this maze to the bottom. If you run into a wall, that's what erasers are for!

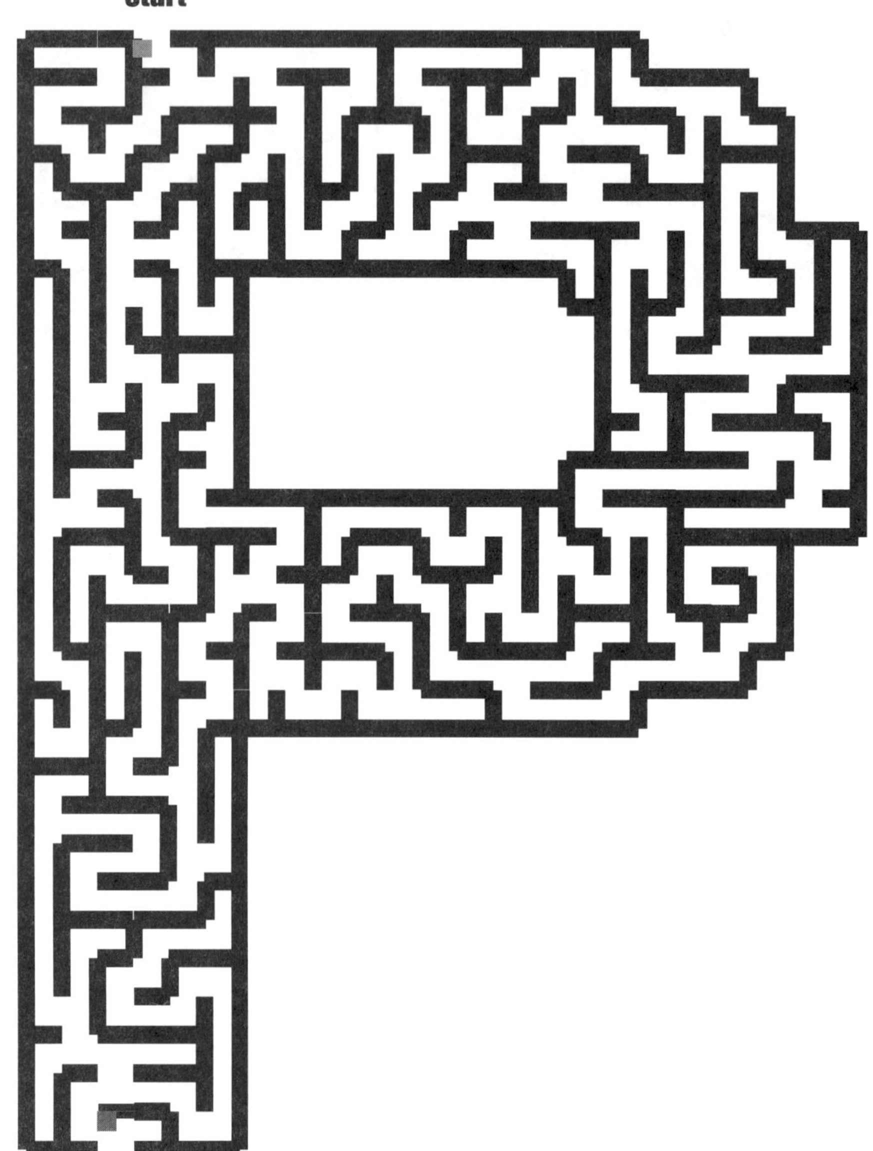

Super Focus: *In your journal, draw a picture of a monster. Make it as frightening as you can. This is your inner critic. It is always there waiting to point out your mistakes. Actually, it's just scared. You can help. Draw a nice room with soft pillows, a window, and stuffed animals. This is your critic's safe place. Next time it says something mean, thank it for trying to help. Then send it to its safe place.*

Name:

Date:

Slaying the Procrastination Dragon: A Project Pacing Page

Congratulations! You have dealt with perfectionism. Now you are ready to face procrastination. It is easier to start an assignment when you know it doesn't have to be perfect, just good.

Facing a big project can feel scary. Creating a plan helps. Divide the work into manageable parts. For example, if you have to read 200 pages and you have 20 days to finish, read 10 pages a day. If you have a month to write a 10-page report, spend 10 days researching, 5 days writing an outline, and 5 days writing a rough draft. Devote the rest of the month to writing the final draft and adding charts or illustrations.

Here's a sample form to get you started:

Class: _________________________ **Period:** __________ **Teacher:** _____________________

Project: ____

Assignment Date: _____________________ **Due Date:** _____________________

Goals/Parts of Project to Complete:

Day (or week) 1: ____

Day (or week) 2: ____

Day (or week) 3: ____

Day (or week) 4: ____

Day (or week) 5: ____

Super Focus: *Small tasks do not require a plan. If you can complete a worksheet in five minutes, do it first. Then, complete assignments that take ten minutes. Finishing a project or a chore offers a feeling of satisfaction and confidence that is hard to replace.*

The best way to overcome procrastination is to get things done. The longer you put off a job, the more overwhelming it seems.

In your journal, draw your procrastination dragon. Write a story about how you tamed it. This can be a very silly tale!

Name:

Date:

Study Time: A Daily To-Do List and Weekly Planner

Finish the shortest assignments first. Savor the satisfaction.

Day (circle one):   M   T   W   Th   F   Date: _______________________

Cross off each assignment when complete.

Period 1 Assignment: ____

Period 2 Assignment: ____

Period 3 Assignment: ____

Period 4 Assignment: ____

Period 5 Assignment: ____

Period 6 Assignment: ____

Questions for a friend, the teacher, or a tutor: _______________________

____

____

Weekly Planner

Ongoing Assignments: ____

Quizzes and tests: ____

Monday: ____

Tuesday: ____

Wednesday: ____

Thursday: ____

Friday: ____

Group Project: ____

Group members and contact information: ______________________________

____

____

My group responsibility this week: __________________________________

____

Abbreviations and Symbols to Use in Notes

- When taking notes, record as much information as possible while listening.
- You are the only one who needs to understand your notes.
- Shorten words and use symbols as much as possible.
- Use bullets, like this, if it helps you separate ideas.

Common symbols used in note taking:

- & or + = and
- e.g. = for example
- i.e. = that is
- ? = maybe, not certain
- X = wrong, incorrect, or avoid
- < = less than or less important than
- > = greater than or more important than
- ✔ = okay or correct
- * = special or very important
- w/ = with; w/o = without
- re = about or regarding
- approx. = approximately
- vs = against or opposing
- stats = statistics

Shorten information in ways you will understand later.
- Leave out vowels. *e.g., you cn prbly ndrstnd ths.*
- Use texting shorthand. *e.g., u already no ABT this. U use abbreviations like B4, BC, POV, AKA, FAQ, ASAP, and NP all the time.* Go ahead, invent your own.
- Use the first few letters of a word such as gov for government, biol for biology, or info for information.
- Use initials for familiar terms such as TOC for Table of Contents, USA, or SCOTUS.
- Leave out unimportant and connecting words. Forget sentences.
- Use arrows to connect ideas unless they confuse you.
- Underline points the teacher says are important. Later, emphasize them with a highlighter.
- Do not abbreviate numbers, dates, new vocabulary, or anything the teacher writes on the board.
- For science, government, history, and grammar, learn standard abbreviations ASAP.

Practice: Go to a streaming site such as YouTube or Vimeo. Find a video about something you are interested in or want to learn. Use abbreviations to take notes. Write down only the most important information. Put your notes away and do something else, then look at them the next day. Can you still understand them? Watch the video again. Did you write down the most important information? If not, change your notes to make them clearer.

Super Focus: *Remember, only you have to understand your notes.*

Name:

Date:

Taking Notes From Nonfiction Reading

Directions for using this form: When reading a textbook, start by checking subheadings, pictures, and diagrams in the chapter. Create a question for each one. Write the questions in the left column. Read for the answer to the first question. Write it in the right column. Don't worry about complete sentences. Abbreviations are fine. Continue to the next question. If the book has no subheadings or pictures, write a question that can be answered by the first page in the chapter. Then, write the answer in your own words.

CLASS _________________ **DATE** ___________ **TEXT** ________________________

TOPIC _________________ **PAGES** ___________

Main Ideas and Questions	**Notes and Answers**

Summary pp. ____

____

Super Focus: *These notes are just for you. They are to help you remember what you read and to help you study for a test later. They can also help you during class discussions.*

Name:

Date:

Taking Notes in Math Class: A Graphic Organizer

Directions for using this form: Work on math problems in the center column. Jot down notes and steps in the right column. Put the main idea of each problem in the left column. Include diagrams or formulas there too. Compare your notes with a friend after class. Ask for help from the teacher if you don't understand.

If your school has a tutoring program, use it. Everybody learns math differently. Individual help can make all the difference.

CLASS _____________ **DATE** _________ **TOPIC** _______________ **TEXT P. #** _______

Main Ideas	Problems	Notes and Steps

Super Focus: Create a reference page with the math formulas you use most often. Making your own chart will help you remember them. Here's an example to get you started. https://www.oregon.gov/ode/educator-resources/assessment/Documents/math_formulapage_gr6-8_eng.pdf

Name:

Date:

Science and Social Studies Notes: A Sample Page

Directions for using this form: Take class notes in the right column. Use abbreviations and symbols you understand. After class, use the left column to summarize each group of ideas. In the left column also include any charts or diagrams, questions you have, and important vocabulary. At the bottom of the page, summarize the whole session.

CLASS: _____________ **DATE:** _________ **TOPIC:** _____________ **TEXT P#_____**

Main Ideas	**Class Notes**

Summary of this Session

Super Focus: *In your binder, create a personal Science Glossary. Add a tab so you can find it quickly. When your teacher introduces an important word in class or you come across one in a reading assignment, add it to your glossary. (A word is important if your teacher writes it on the board or it is printed in **bold type** in the text.)*

Name: _______________________________   Date: _______________________________

Story Analyzer: A Graphic Organizer for Literature

Directions: Use a form like this to prepare for a class discussion about a novel or short story.

Book Title: ____

Author: ____

Characters:

- Main Character: ____

    o Sidekick Characters: ____

- Opposition Character: ____

    o Sidekick Characters: ____

Setting (Time and Place): ____

Point of View (circle one): 1st Person   2nd Person   3rd Person   Multiple viewpoints

Problem (What does the main character want or need?): ____________________

____

Opposition (What keeps the main character from succeeding?)

- Obstacle 1: ____

- Obstacle 2: ____

- Obstacle 3: ____

Resolution (Is the problem solved? If so, how?): _________________________

____

How does the main character grow or change? ____________________________

____

Theme (e.g., love, greed, friendship, adventure, identity, courage): ____________

Literary Devices (page # and example):

Simile (page # ______): ____

Metaphor (page # ______): ____

Personification (page # ______): ____

Foreshadowing (page # ______): ____

Flashback (page # ______): ____

My favorite part of the story was _______________________________________

If I had written this story, I would have changed _______________________

____

Questions to ask: ____

____

Name:

Date:

Taking Great Notes: A Word Search

Directions: Find and circle the words related to note-taking in the word search puzzle. Answers may be printed forward or backward, horizontally, vertically, or diagonally.

Abbreviations	Active	Arrows	Ask	Attention	Box
Bullet	Charts	Circle	Codes	Columns	Compare
Concentration	Critical	Facts	Formulas	Ideas	Important
Listening	Main	Memory	Organization	Questions	Rewording
Steps	Study	Summaries	Thinking	Underline	Vocabulary

```
S N M U L O C Y U N Z R C V J Q V P M
A M C W E R A P M O C O D E S N O J L
B O F B B U R Y C H N S S O M V C I C
B G W Z U B S D K C U J X X Z P A D X
R C L I L Y Q V E M K B O X M X B C H
E I X D L O Z N M G A C T I V E U R A
V R H E E D T A S W G T U X A U L I E
I C F A T R R G T I N S T Q H O A T N
A L L S A I N Y C P I T Q E S P R I I
T E H T E I P U A S N R U B N Y Y C L
I R I S K Q C H F A E A E U N T V A R
O O K N J G L N T L T H S S O R I L E
N F I B J X H R S U S C T B S H U O D
S H J N Q M O S P M I M I B J T C X N
T W G N E P W E E R L E O M M M U C U
N I B M M O T Z T O J T N E N A Z D T
J D O I R Q P I S F O I S F O I I K Y
M R O R G A N I Z A T I O N C N A C S
Y L A R E W O R D I N G A S K Q Y Q I
```

Super Focus: *List three ways taking good notes helps you focus or three reasons note-taking is confusing for you. If you find note-taking distracting, ask your teacher or tutor for help.*

Planning Stories and Essays

Planning a Short Story

Use these questions to structure your story. Some writers answer one or two of the questions and then write a quick first draft. They find other answers as they go. Others use questions like this to make an outline. Experiment. Find the way that works best for you.

- Whose story is this? (Main character)
- Is the story told in 1st or 3rd person? (*I* or *name/he/she*)
- Where and when does the story take place?
- Is the story told in the present or past tense?
- What is the problem?
- How does the character feel about the problem?
- How does the character try to solve the problem?
- Who or what prevents the character from solving the problem? (Hint, the more powerful this opposition, the more interesting the story will be.) In many stories, the character tries two times and fails.
- How does the character finally solve the problem?
- How does the character change because of this adventure?

Planning an Essay

You can find templates for planning essays online. They tell you what to include in each paragraph. Artificial intelligence bots can write essays like that. Here's a way to help you write an essay that only you can compose.

- What is the topic or question?
- What is your opinion about the topic?
- Why do you feel that way? (Include relevant personal experiences.)
  - o Reason 1:
  - o Reason 2:
  - o Reason 3:
- What sources agree with you and why? (Consult  books, search online, take a survey, and/or ask people with relevant experience.)
  - o Source 1:
  - o Source 2:
  - o Source 3:
- What are the arguments against your point of view?
  - o Argument 1:
    - ■ Your answer
  - o Argument 2:
    - ■ Your answer
  - o Argument 3:
    - ■ Your answer
- Repeat your opinion and summarize your reasons for holding it, in spite of arguments against it.

Name:

Date:

Enjoying Discussions: A Crossword Puzzle

Directions: Complete the crossword puzzle with words related to having a classroom discussion. The number in parentheses indicates how many letters are in the word.

Across

3. Make your _________ clearly. (6)
5. _________ relevant personal experiences. (5)
9. _________ everyone in the group. (7)
11. Keep an _________ mind. (4)
12. Stay on the _________. (5)
13. _________ or rephrase what the last speaker said. (6)
14. Let everyone have a _________ to speak. (4)
15. It is often better to _________ and listen than to rush to speak. (4)

Down

1. Take _________ on points others make. (5)
2. _________ when others speak. (6)
3. To take part in something is to _________. (11)
4. _________ by doing the reading in advance. (7)
6. _________ when it is your turn. (5)
7. Be ready to _________ your arguments. (7)
8. Keep your _________ on the topic. (5)
10. Pay _________ to what others say. (9)

Name: Date:

Short Break Activities and Snacks: A Brainstormer

Short breaks make your study sessions much more efficient.

Directions: Take a few minutes to list ideas for five-minute and twenty-minute breaks. Choose things you enjoy. They should not require a lot of equipment or preparation. Keep this list handy in your study space.

Five-Minute Break Activities

______________________________   ______________________________

______________________________   ______________________________

______________________________   ______________________________

______________________________   ______________________________

______________________________   ______________________________

Twenty-Minute Break Activities

______________________________   ______________________________

______________________________   ______________________________

______________________________   ______________________________

______________________________   ______________________________

Focus Snacks
Take time to research healthy snacks. List your favorites here. Prepare some in advance and keep them handy.

______________________________   ______________________________

______________________________   ______________________________

______________________________   ______________________________

______________________________   ______________________________

Name: Date:

Escape Anxiety With Concentration:
A Mandala Coloring Page

Mandalas are complex symmetrical designs. Coloring them carefully takes concentration. When you work on them you can't think about anything else. They improve focus and help you relax. You can find them in special coloring books. They are also available online.

Super Focus: *Many offline activities that require concentration can help you relax and improve your ability to focus. Musical instrument practice, puzzles, running, and reading are just a few possibilities.*

For optimum mental and physical health, limit your use of electronic devices. Playing with them sometimes is fun, but they are designed to be addictive. Stay in charge of your time and attention.

Name: ___________________

Date: ___________________

My Monthly Gratitude Tracker

Taking a minute at the end of each day to find something to be grateful for makes a huge difference for some people. Try it every night for a month. If it works for you, add a gratitude box to each page of your journal.

Month: ___________________

Day:

1 ___________________
2 ___________________
3 ___________________
4 ___________________
5 ___________________
6 ___________________
7 ___________________
8 ___________________
9 ___________________
10 ___________________
11 ___________________
12 ___________________
13 ___________________
14 ___________________
15 ___________________
16 ___________________
17 ___________________
18 ___________________
19 ___________________
20 ___________________
21 ___________________
22 ___________________
23 ___________________
24 ___________________
25 ___________________
26 ___________________
27 ___________________
28 ___________________
29 ___________________
30 ___________________
31 ___________________

Name: ____________________   Date: ____________________

Positive Self-talk and Other Study Superchargers: A Crossword Puzzle

Directions: Complete the crossword puzzle with words that complete the positive statements below. The number in parentheses indicates how many letters are in the word.

Across

1. I _______ strong and resilient. (2)
2. I can choose how to _______ to any situation. (5)
4. I am taking care of _______ body. (2)
7. I stand _______ for myself. (2)
8. I can handle this _______. (9)
11. I _______ the feelings of others. (7)
13. I am _______ for my body. (8)
15. I am proud of my _______. (15)
20. I am willing to ask for _______. (4)
21. I am proud of _______ I am. (3)
23. I can find _______ solutions. (8)
24. I deserve time for _______ and fun. (10)
25. I am _______ and will not give up. (10)
26. I am patient _______ myself. (4)
27. I deserve to _______. (7)
29. When others give me _______, I use it to improve. (8)
30. I am confident in my _______. (9)
32. I _______ to be happy. (7)

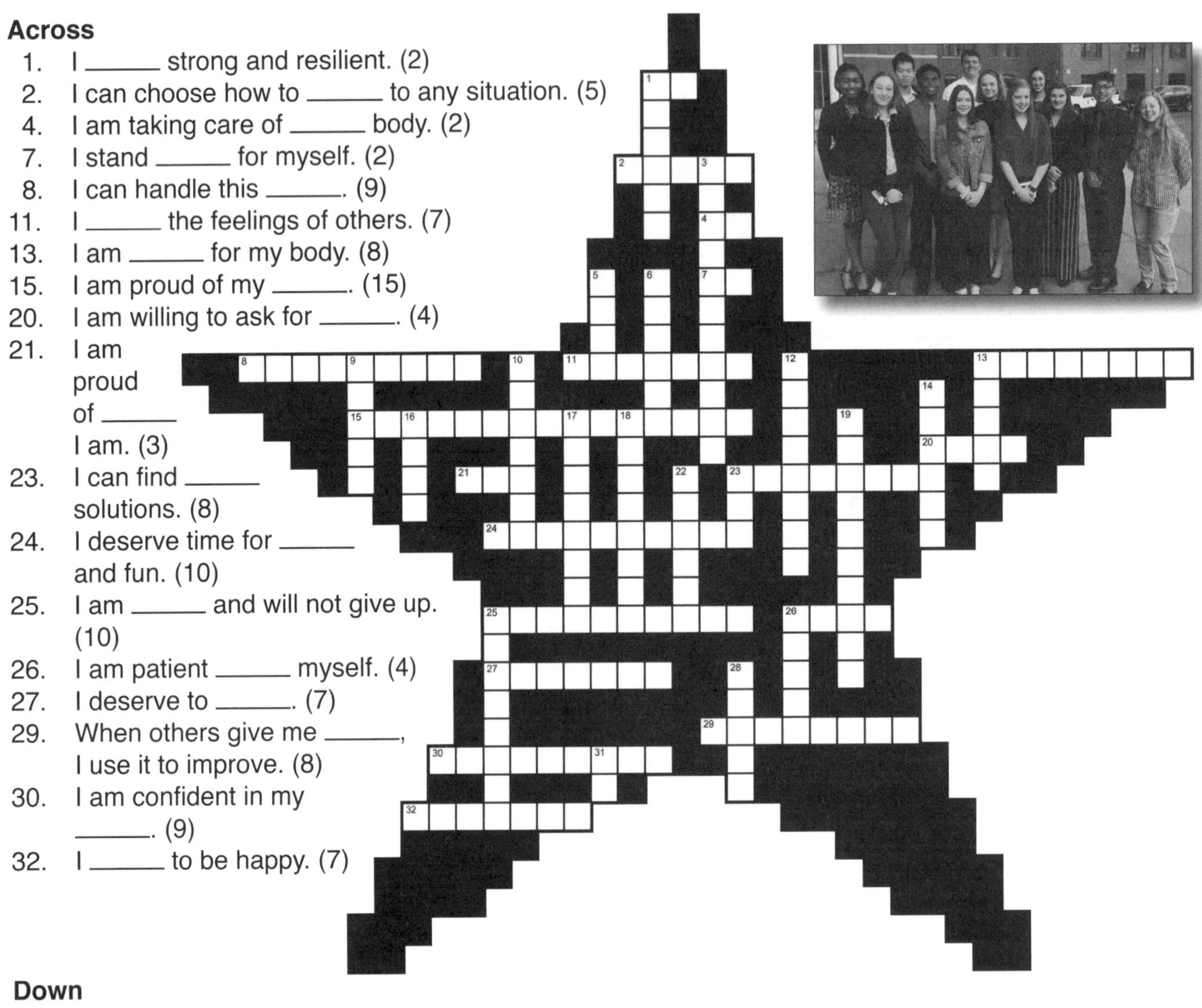

Down

1. I _______ myself just as I am. (6)
3. I can _______ my thoughts to others. (11)
5. I will _______ smart decisions. (4)
6. I surround myself with _______ who appreciate me. (6)
9. I _______ from mistakes. (5)
10. When difficulties occur, I _______ them as ways to grow. (7)
12. I am a good _______. (8)
13. I am taking steps toward my _______. (5)
14. I treat _______ with kindness. (6)
16. I am _______ under stress. (4)
17. I bounce back from _______. (8)
18. My _______ help me grow. (8)
19. I am _______ about the future. (10)
22. I have _______ strengths and talents. (6)
23. I _______ overcome obstacles (3)
25. I focus on my _______ qualities. (8)
26. I will make a difference in the _______. (5)
28. I make the most of _______ opportunity. (5)
31. I am _______ control of my feelings. (2)

Bullet Journaling

A bullet journal is a tool to help you make friends with yourself.

Different people use these journals in different ways, but no matter how you use it, this little notebook is just for you. It is a map to help you keep track of where you are in your life. Once set up, it should be easy and fun to use.

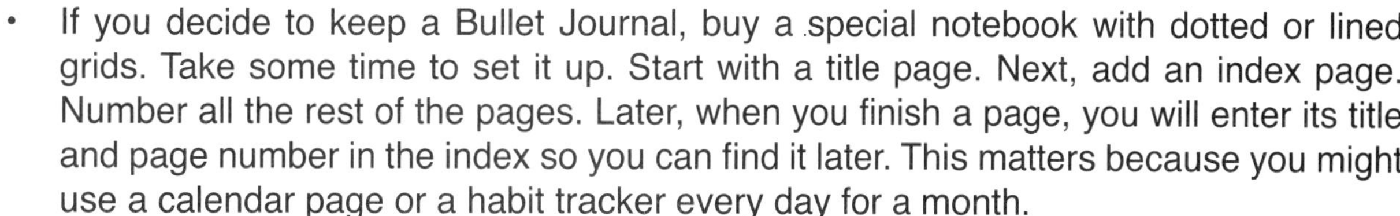

- Start with a few individual pages to see if you like the process.
- Use the dots to guide your ruler when you divide a page into sections.
- Fine-tipped colored pens, pencils, or markers make bullet journaling more fun, but start with what you have.
- Look online, especially on Pinterest, for more samples and ideas. Search for "Bullet Journals for Middle School Students."
- If you decide to keep a Bullet Journal, buy a special notebook with dotted or lined grids. Take some time to set it up. Start with a title page. Next, add an index page. Number all the rest of the pages. Later, when you finish a page, you will enter its title and page number in the index so you can find it later. This matters because you might use a calendar page or a habit tracker every day for a month.
- Date all your pages.

Ideas for bullet journal pages include:
- Seven Days of Gratitude: One or two things you are grateful for each day of the week
- A custom daily, weekly, or monthly calendar (Most official Bullet Journals are centered around all three kinds of calendars, but you don't have to use yours this way.)
- A daily to-do or things-done list
- A brain dump for the day—short jottings or pictures about things on your mind
- A dreams and goals list
- A yearly record of books read with personal star ratings and brief notes
- Personal address, phone number, email, and social media contact pages
- Questions to ask or research
- Inspiring quotations or affirmations
- A habit tracker:
  - Title the page.
  - Create a box for each day of the month.
  - Did you follow the improved habit? Use a check for yes and a blank for no.
  - Choose just one habit to track.
  - **Important!** This is just to make you aware of what you are doing. Keep track, but it's okay if you slip up.
  - You might track things like
    - 9 hours of sleep
    - healthy breakfast, lunch, or dinner
    - remembered school supplies or assignments

Super Focus: Notice that you track positive new habits, not the old bad ones.

Name:

Date:

A Practice Bullet Journal Page

Directions: Decide what you want to track or record on this page. Give it a title. Then, divide it into two or three boxes or rectangles. Use the dots to guide your ruler. Use one section for a quotation or an inspiring word. Add some doodles, a sticker, or a stamp.

Name:

Date:

Mindfulness: A Crossword Puzzle

Directions: Complete the crossword puzzle with words related to mindfulness. The number in parentheses indicates how many letters are in the word.

Across

1. enjoying an experience, such as a meal (8)
5. the ability to bounce back (10)
6. thankfulness (9)
8. awareness of the feelings of others (7)
9. air taken into the body or released (6)
12. being alone (8)
16. something to pay without money (9)
17. a purpose that guides decisions (9)
18. No sound (7)
19. No movement (9)

Down

2. to build back (7)
3. paying full attention to any experience (7)
4. the quality of keeping an open mind (8)
7. to breathe in (6)
10. embracing the reality of the moment (10)
11. focusing the mind to achieve a sense of calm (10)
13. being in the now instead of the past or future; the _____ of mind (8)
14. the ability to wait (8)
15. positive feelings toward others; also a thrift store (8)

Resources for Students: Books, Websites, and Organizations

Books:

Breathe Like a Bear: 30 Mindful Moments for Kids to Feel Calm and Focused Anytime, Anywhere by Kira Willey

The Everything Guide to Study Skills: Strategies, Tips, and Tools You Need to Succeed in School! by Cynthia C. Muchnick

The Focused Mind: 42 Powerful Tips to Help You Focus, Concentrate, and Achieve Success by Gabriel Dee

The Middle School Student's Guide to Ruling the World! by Susan Mulcaire

Train Your Brain for Success: A Teenager's Guide to Executive Functions by Randy Kulman

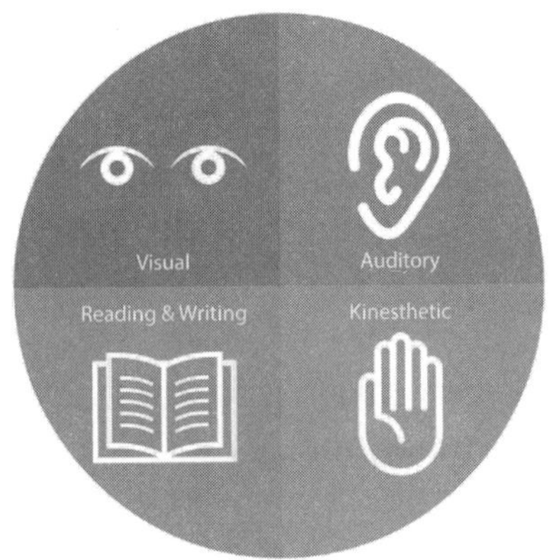

Websites:

"12 Surprising Study and Test Skills for Middle and High Schoolers" – These tested strategies on the *Made for Math* site work for all subjects. <https://madeformath.com/study-skills/>

"Crash Course" – This channel offers lessons on science, history, literature, and more. The site's videos make hard subjects more understandable and interesting. <https://www.youtube.com/user/crashcourse>

"Focus and Concentration Games"— Looking for something to do during a brain break? *Improve Memory.org* offers a dizzying variety of online games. <https://www.improvememory.org/focus-concentration-games/>

"GoZen!" – This site offers games, animations, and exercises to help with anxiety. <https://www.gozen.com/>

"Monday Mandala"— 216 beautiful mandalas are available on this site to download and print. A great way to take a break and relax. <https://mondaymandala.com/m/>

"Quizlet" – Visit this platform to create flashcards and study sets. It offers games and practice tests to help you review. <https://quizlet.com/>

"Smiling Mind"– This free mindfulness app and website offers guided meditations and mindfulness activities. Use it to reduce stress and improve focus. <https://www.smilingmind.com.au/>

Answer Key

Find the Feelings: An Emotion Word Search (page 32)

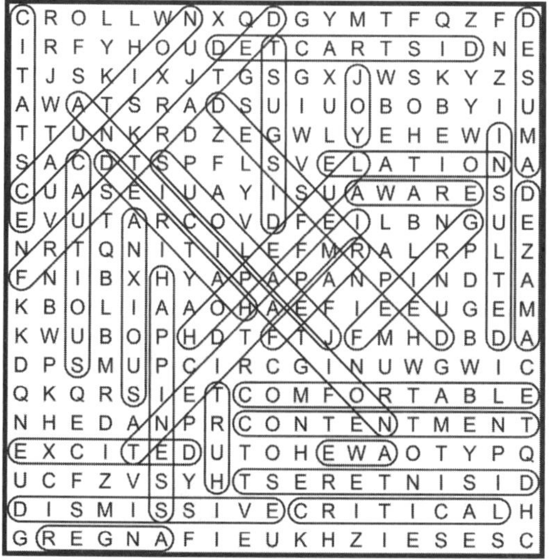

Distracto Destructo: A Dot-to-Dot Puzzle (page 34)

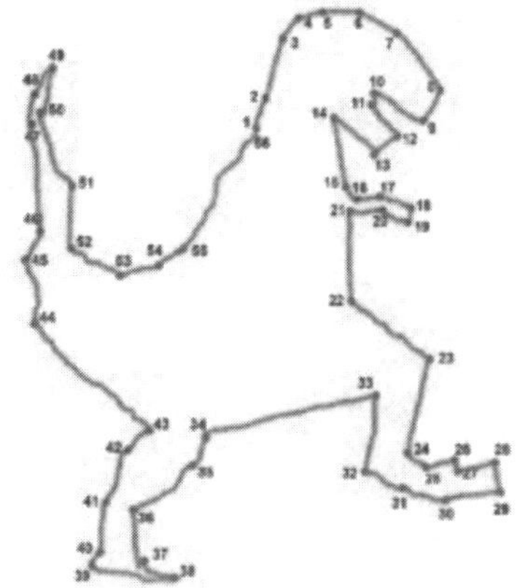

Distraction-Busters: A Word Search (page 35)

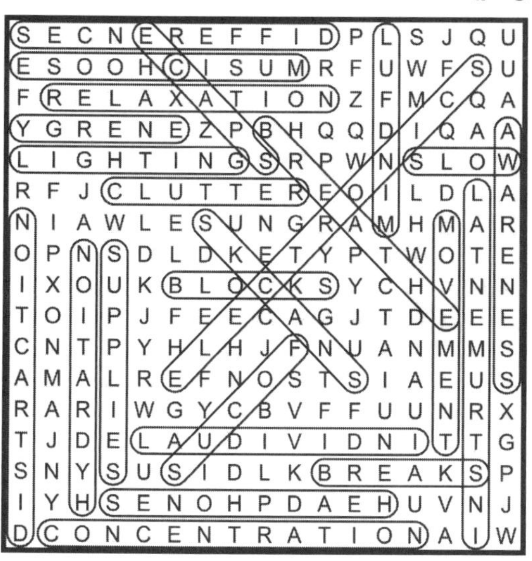

Brain Foods: A Crossword Puzzle (page 36)

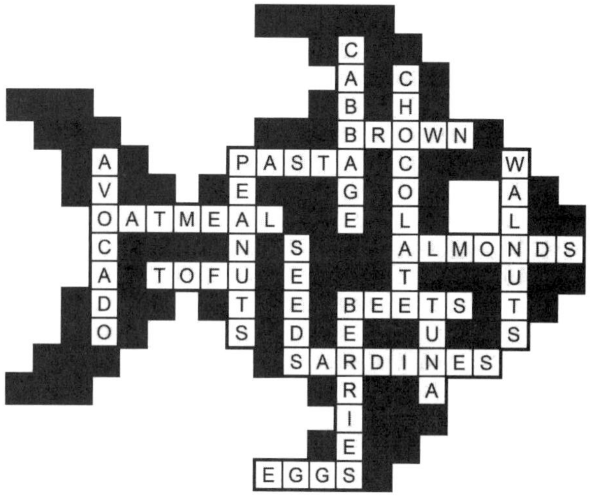

Sleep for Success: A Crossword Puzzle (page 39)

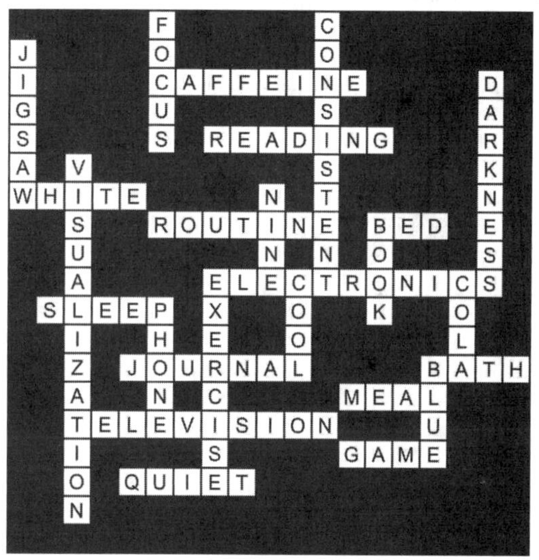

P is for Perfectionism: A Maze (page 40)

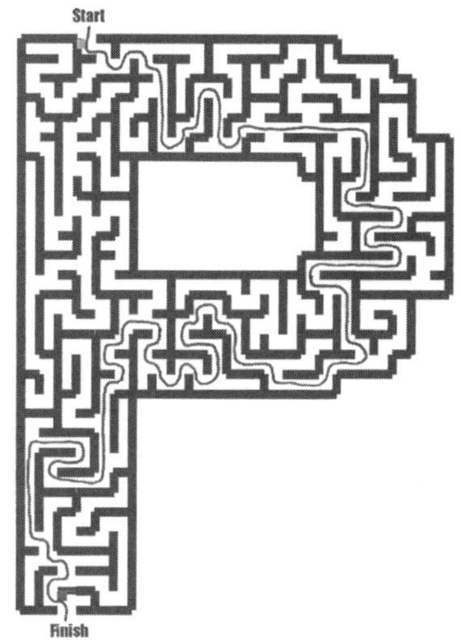

Answer Key (cont.)

Taking Great Notes: A Word Search (page 48)

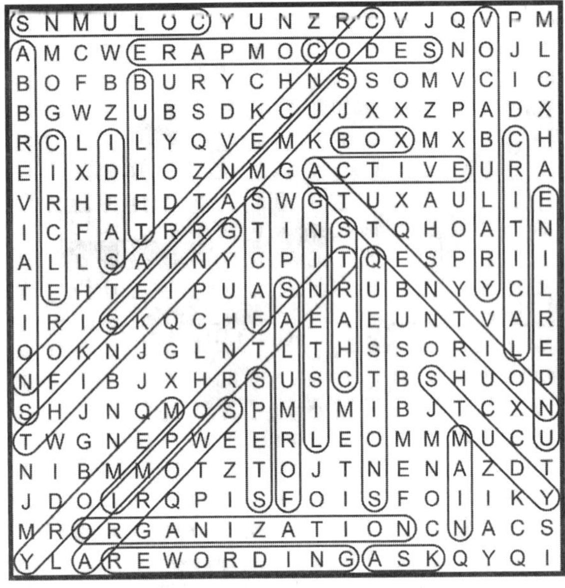

Positive Self-Talk and Other Study Superchargers: A Crossword Puzzle (page 54)

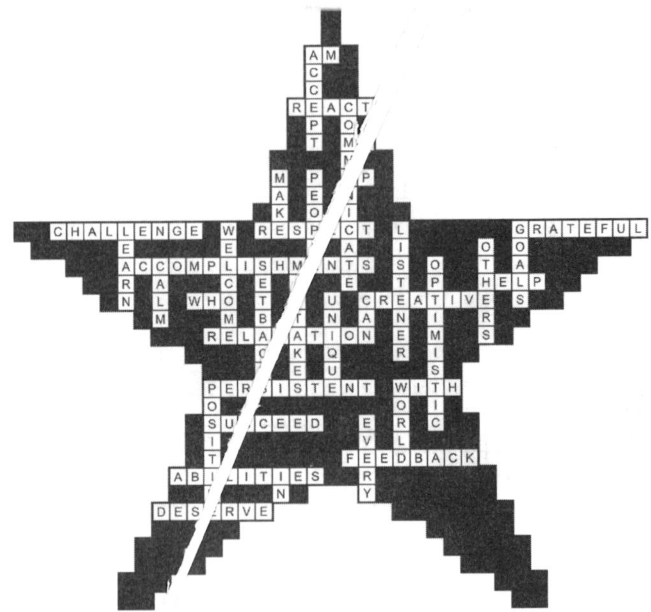

Enjoying Discussions: A Crossword Puzzle (page 50)

Mindfulness: A Crossword Puzzle (page 57)

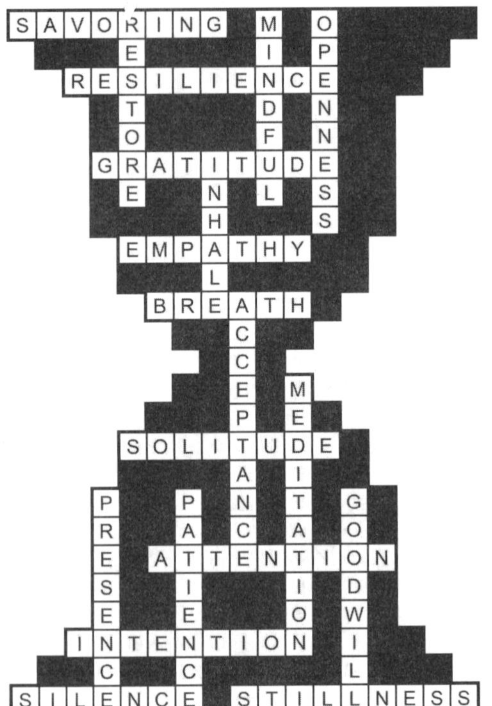